SAN FRANCISCO

A PHOTOGRAPHIC PORTRAIT

PHOTOGRAPHY BY

Bob Morris

NARRATIVE BY

Joslyn Hamilton

TWIN LIGHTS PUBLISHERS, ROCKPORT, MASSACHUSETTS

First published in the United States of America by:

Twin Lights Publishers, Inc.
51 Broadway
Rockport, Massachusetts 01966
Telephone: (978) 546-7398
www.twinlightspub.com

ISBN: 978-1-934907-31-3

10 9 8 7 6 5 4 3 2 1

(opposite)
Golden Gate Bridge

(*frontispiece*)
Transamerica Building
and Sentinel Building

(*jacket front*)
Golden Gate Bridge

Book design by:
SYP Design & Production, Inc.
www.sypdesign.com

Printed in China

A magnet for iconoclasts and adventure seekers, San Francisco is a city with a rich history that includes settlement by the Ohlone Indians, Spanish missionaries, Mexican colonizers, European gold seekers, and Asian immigrants. All came in search of a new life in a better place; San Francisco still holds the allure of a better life for the tens of thousands who move to the city every year.

"The City by the Bay" has the distinction of being the only city in the state of California that is its own self-contained county. Situated on a peninsula bound by water on three sides, the city measures 46.9 square miles, or roughly seven by seven miles—a relatively small urban area with plenty to love. San Francisco is an incredibly diverse place, known for its open-minded and free-spirited ethos. Inclusion has always been a priority for San Franciscans, and creativity a championed quality—as illustrated by the many outdoor artworks scattered around the various neighborhoods and the festivals and events that take place year-round in the mild climate of the Bay Area.

Long before California became part of the Union, San Francisco was settled by colonists from Spain and named after their beloved St. Francis of Assisi, who abandoned his taste for the worldly life after a vision that inspired him to live simply, without material attachment. San Francisco's first European mission—which still stands in the aptly-named Mission District—was Mission San Francisco de Asís, otherwise known as Mission Dolores. Eventually, San Francisco gained independence from Spain and was annexed by Mexico, and the town was renamed Yerba Buena, after a local aromatic mint plant, before officially becoming San Francisco in 1776—seventy-four years before California's official induction into the United States.

Unlike St. Francis, San Francisco's European settlers were indeed motivated by riches as they migrated west during the Gold Rush. Over the centuries, San Francisco has been a revolutionary hotbed for plenty of other renegades as well, from the racy Barbary Coast characters to the Beat Generation and the hippies who put Haight-Ashbury on the map and launched the career of the Grateful Dead.

The progressive spirit of counterculture is still alive and well in San Francisco; today, it's epitomized by Burning Man and the many tech startups revolutionizing our modern lifestyle. The bold, adventurous spirit of gold-seeking prospectors is still a prominent part of San Francisco's culture, and the city remains a destination for the best and brightest creative, cultural, and technical minds.

Fountain of the Tortoises *(opposite)*

The centerpiece of Nob Hill's Huntington Park is a replica of the *Fontana delle Tartarughe*, designed in 1581 by Giacomo della Porta and still standing in Rome. San Francisco's version was commissioned by William H. and Ethel Crocker and later gifted to the city by their children.

Yerba Buena Gardens

Named after the city's original Mexican settlement, Yerba Buena Gardens spans two verdant blocks connected by a pedestrian bridge. It is home to a landscaped esplanade, a center for the arts, an ice-skating rink, an old-fashioned carousel, and several other attractions.

Cupid's Span

Brazenly displayed in Rincon Park along the Embarcadero, *Cupid's Span* is a 60-foot-tall fiberglass and stainless-steel sculpture designed by Claes Oldenburg and Coosje van Bruggen. The sculpture's silhouette suggests a ship sailing the Bay, its heart firmly in San Francisco.

Financial District

Virtually destroyed in the earthquake and fire of 1906, the city's downtown business district was eventually rebuilt with picturesque low-rise brick buildings and neo-Gothic high-rises that now define the city's financial center, snugly situated along the Embarcadero on the San Francisco Bay.

Admission Day Monument

At the intersection of Market and Montgomery streets, in the heart of the downtown business district, it's easy to spot this 1897 sculpture by Douglas Tilden, designed to commemorate California's induction into the Union and still standing after the earthquake and fire of 1906.

Embarcadero *(above)*

Spanish for "place to embark," the palm-lined Embarcadero was once the main route through the bustling seaport of the early 20th century. The avenue fell into decline when the Bay Bridge was built and boat traffic shifted, but was spectacularly restored in the 1990s.

Annular Eclipse *(opposite)*

Installed in 2000, George Rickey's kinetic sculpture *Annular Eclipse* is a cheeky ode to nature juxtaposed against the city skyline. Mechanically rotating silver disks cross each other to mimic an annular eclipse, when the moon crosses the sun to reveal only a bright ring of light.

690

Lotta's Fountain *(opposite)*

Affectionately considered an eyesore by many locals, this cast-iron fountain stands as a testament to the city's enduring spirit. After the great earthquake and fire of 1906, the fountain served as a meeting point for survivors, and commemorative gatherings are still held here every year.

The Mechanics *(above)*

San Francisco's "Father of Sculpture," Douglas Tilden, designed *The Mechanics* statue to feature five nude men, which caused a stir. It was nearly dismantled, but a group of local artists won a petition for it to stand, and stand it did, even through the great earthquake of 1906.

San Francisco City Hall *(top)*

City Hall has been pivotal to the city's gay rights movement since Mayor Moscone and Supervisor Harvey Milk were assassinated here in 1978. Now, along with many other civic duties, gay marriages are held every day in this exquisitely designed beaux-arts building.

City Hall West Side Door *(bottom)*

City Hall was built in 1899, rebuilt after the earthquake of 1906, damaged again in the earthquake of 1989, and renovated in 1999 to the existing seismic-proof edifice. Designed in the beaux-arts style, much of its beauty lies in the details—like this ornately gilded door.

The City Hall Dome *(opposite)*

City Hall's dome, the fifth largest in the world, sheds a golden gleam on Van Ness Avenue. Twisted a full four inches off its base in the 1989 Loma Prieta earthquake, it has since been fully restored and is now outfitted with multi-colored LED lighting to celebrate special occasions.

Grand Staircase, City Hall *(left)*

Many of City Hall's memories are formed on the Grand Staircase, where newly wedded straight and gay couples pose daily for photographs, and where 1960s protesters once rallied together to voice their concerns over hearings by the House Un-American Activities Committee.

Harvey Milk Bust *(right)*

Harvey Milk, the first openly gay person elected to public office in California, was assassinated by City Supervisor Dan White in City Hall in 1978. Nearly three decades later, a bronze bust was erected at the top of the Grand Staircase to memorialize this iconic civil rights leader.

Federal Reserve Bank *(opposite)*

The city's Federal Reserve Bank represents nine western states and has one of the largest collections of U.S. paper money in the country. In 1983, the bank moved from its previous location on Sansome Street to occupy this modern, energy-efficient building on Market Street.

FEDERAL RESERVE BANK
SAN FRANCISCO

U.S. Mint *(above)*

The old U.S. Mint building, often called "The Granite Lady"—somewhat of a misnomer, since it's constructed mostly of sandstone—was sold to the city by the federal government for a silver dollar and is slated to become the permanent home of the Museum of the City of San Francisco.

U.S. Mint's Portico *(left)*

The old U.S. Mint on Fifth Street is a gargantuan stone building styled like an ancient Greek temple, with a central portico supported by imposing round columns. The building survived the earthquake of 1906 while everything around it crumbled. However, it was eventually forsaken for a bigger, more modern facility.

Civic Center

A National Historic Landmark, San Francisco's Civic Center has seen its share of history and is often the site of political protests, rallies, and civic celebrations. Its buildings include City Hall (shown), the Bill Graham Civic Auditorium, the Herbst Theatre, and the city's main library.

California Palace of the Legion of Honor *(above and left)*

An outpost of the city's Fine Arts Museums' network, the Legion of Honor is perched on a hill in Lincoln Park. It holds a collection of 4,000 years of ancient and European art, including its prize piece, Rodin's *Thinker*, and one of the country's largest compilations of prints and drawings.

Martin Luther King Memorial

(opposite, top and bottom)

Illuminated at night, a fifty-foot-wide wall of cascading water flows in front of a walkway under a 120,000-gallon reflecting pool in the Yerba Buena Center. Light plays off glass panels along the walkway, where etched quotes from King's speeches are translated into 13 languages, an inclusive experience for any visitor.

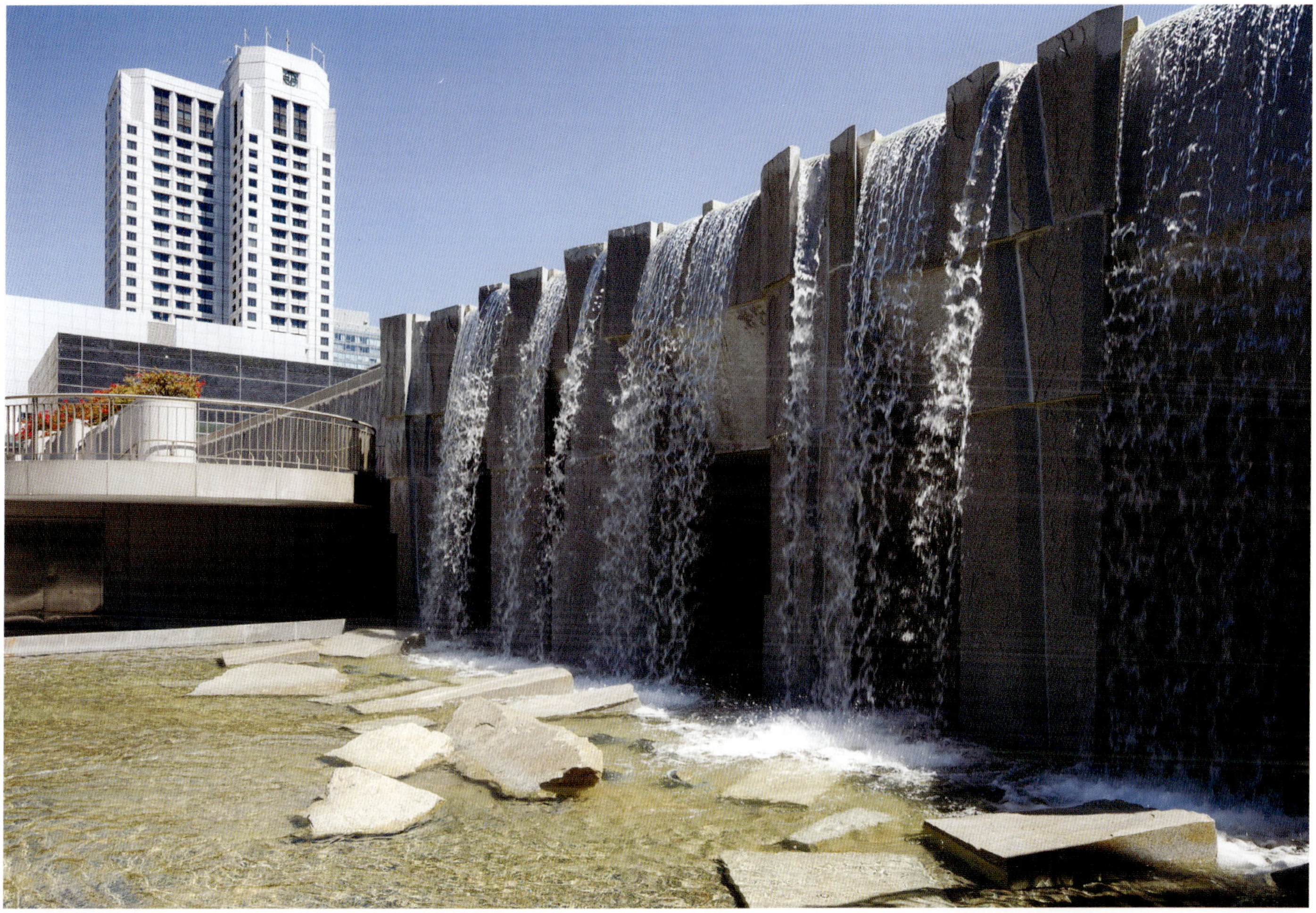

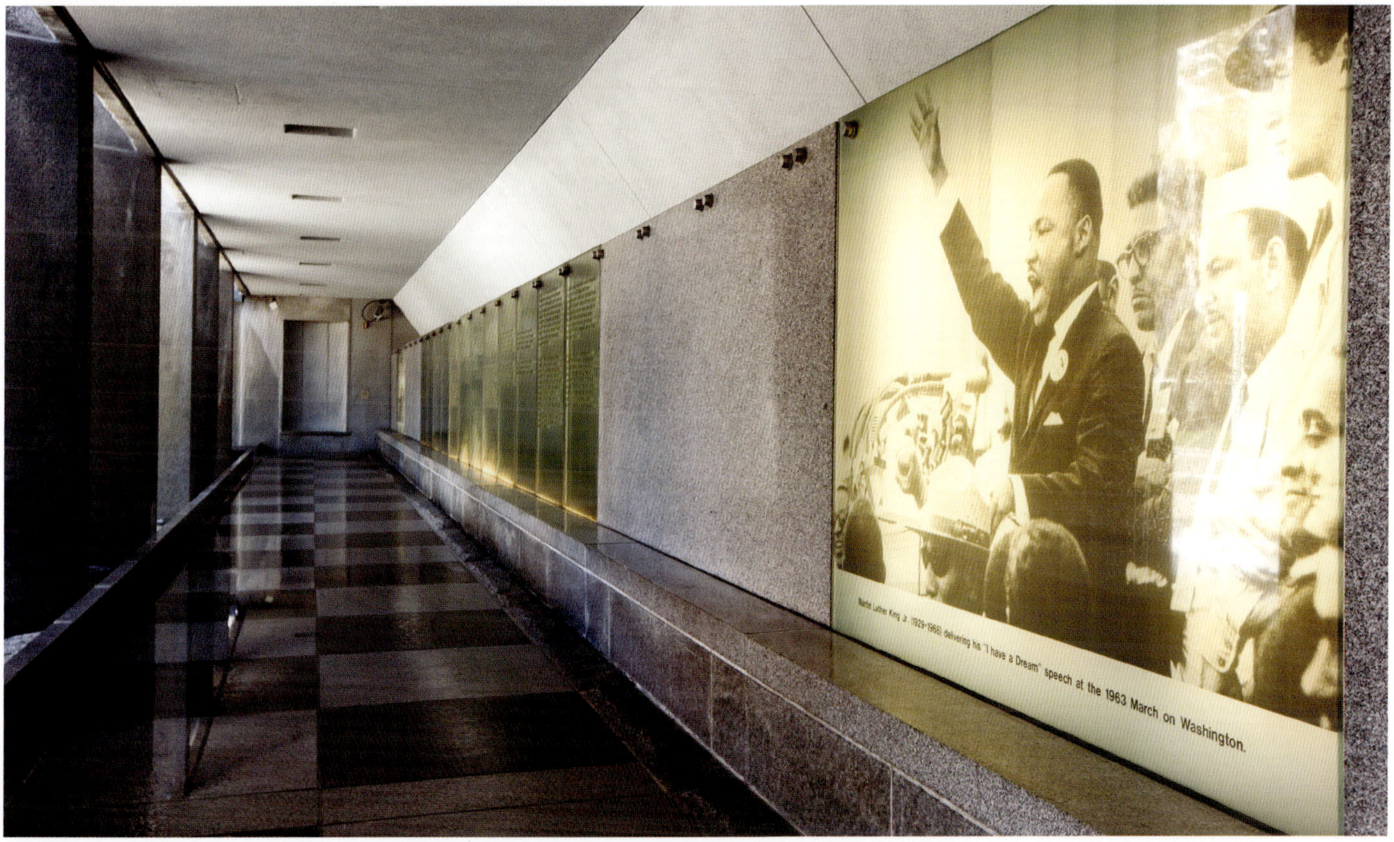
Martin Luther King Jr. (1929-1968) delivering his "I have a Dream" speech at the 1963 March on Washington.

Murals of Coit Tower *(top and bottom)*

Coit Tower's narrative fresco murals, created in the 1930s by local Bay Area artists, tell stories of the state's colorful culture and history in great detail. The historic murals were considered quite controversial at the time they were installed.

Coit Tower *(opposite)*

The Lillie Coit Memorial Tower stands only 210 feet tall but lords gracefully over the northern part of the city from Telegraph Hill's peak. The art deco tower was erected as part of a 1930s beautification effort, using funds from the estate of eccentric benefactor Lillie Hitchcock Coit.

Crissy Field *(above)*

Close to the Golden Gate Bridge at the northern tip of the city is Crissy Field, once a U.S. Army airfield and now part of Golden Gate National Recreation Area. Its bayside walking trail and wooden pier are filled with tourists and fitness-minded locals walking, jogging, and biking.

Crissy Field Sculptures *(opposite)*

This spunky exhibit is well situated in care-free Crissy Field. Artist Mark di Suvero worked with the SFMOMA, the National Park Service, and Golden Gate National Parks to install his eight large-scale red steel sculptures against the matching backdrop of the Golden Gate Bridge.

Coastal Trail

The California Coastal Trail is an ongoing project to connect the state's entire 1,200-mile coastline. It meanders along the bluffs of the Pacific at the western boundary of the city, from the Sutro Baths all the way north to the Golden Gate Bridge, passing several somewhat secluded city beaches.

Sutro Baths

A century ago, San Franciscans could take their pick of seven swimming pools, see a concert, or go ice skating at Sutro Baths, the world's largest indoor pool complex. The ruins of these decadent baths, which were destroyed by fire in the 1960s, are managed by the National Park Service.

Alcatraz

One of San Francisco's most thrilling activities is visiting Alcatraz Island, once a maximum-security prison island known as "the Rock," where the worst of the worst convicts were sent to languish in plain site of the city. Now, Alcatraz is a quick ferry ride and a fascinating historical experience.

Wave Organ

Nestled on a man-made jetty outlining Boat Harbor, the *Wave Organ* is an acoustic sculpture constructed from 25 organ pipes that amplify sound as the tides rise and fall. Artists Peter Richards and George Gonzalez built stone platforms where visitors listen to the melody of the Bay.

Fort Point

The guardian of the Golden Gate, Fort Point was built to protect the city from Confederate and foreign naval attack, but no shot was ever fired from its garrison. One hundred and fifty years later, the handsome masonry still stands; the bridge's base was built to accommodate it.

San Francisco Bay *(above)*

With spectacular views of Alcatraz Island, Angel Island, the golden Marin Headlands, and Aquatic Park, San Francisco Bay is not only a busy boat route from the open sea to the Port of Oakland, but one of the city's most popular recreation spots.

Golden Gate Bridge *(pages 32 – 33)*

The view of the Golden Gate Bridge from the Marin Headlands, north of the city, will take your breath away. Here, you can view the Mediterranean-white span of the cityscape through the "international orange" towers of San Francisco's beloved suspension bridge, built in 1937.

Pier 39

Families with children get the most bang for their buck at this tourist attraction built on a pier in Fisherman's Wharf. Stores, restaurants, the Aquarium of the Bay, and a two-story carousel compete with countless street performers and extroverted sea lions vying for attention.

Ferries of Pier 39 *(top)*

From Pier 39, one can catch a five-minute boat taxi to nearby Forbes Island, a floating restaurant designed to look like a tropical island with a lighthouse and real palm trees, or all the way to Alcatraz, Angel Island, Alameda, or Sausalito on one of several frequent ferries.

Sea Lions of Pier 39 *(bottom)*

Whether they're hungry for attention or the plentiful food in the Bay waters, hordes of male sea lions have claimed Pier 39 as their home ever since the Loma Prieta earthquake of 1989. Now a tourist attraction, these playful lions can number upwards of 1700 on the pier.

San Francisco Carousel *(above)*

Central to the Pier 39 promenade, this two-tier carousel, hand-painted with favorite local landmarks, was imported from Italy. A spin on a galloping horse or rocking chariot is accompanied by traditional organ music and, at night, the illumination of 1,800 LED lights.

Shops of Pier 39 *(opposite)*

For tourists in search of a San Francisco keepsake, the shops along the promenade on Pier 39 offer everything from charms to chocolates. Visit the Alcatraz and Aquarium of the Bay gift shops, the Cable Car Store, or the San Francisco Sock Market for a quirky city memento.

OUT OF THE BOX
HARRY MASON
DESIGN STUDIO
GAMES
THINK OUT OF THE BOX
PUZZLES
NFL Shop
COFFEE • CUPCAKES •
illy
Cup&Cake café
CREPES
FRENCH CREPES
BREAKFAST
WILDER WEST
THE CABLE CAR STORE

Dining at Fisherman's Wharf

The taste of the sea is alive and well in San Francisco's historic fishing district, with the wide range of mouth-watering options including walk-up oyster bars and upscale eateries with a romantic Bay view—like Alioto's, which has served traditional Sicilian seafood since 1925.

Fisherman's Wharf

Before its renovation into a trendy tourist attraction in the 1970s, Fisherman's Wharf was (and still is) home to San Francisco's fishing fleet. Year round, tourists throng the streets and piers to enjoy delicious seafood—notably the Dungeness crab that the wharf was built for.

Dungeness Crabs *(opposite and top)*

Fisherman's Wharf is famous for its fresh seafood, and seasonal Dungeness crab is perhaps the most popular catch of all. In late fall, fisherman steam the big, golden-red crabs right on the street. Most are now trapped beyond the Golden Gate Bridge near the protected Farallon Islands.

Ghirardelli Square *(bottom)*

When San Franciscans think "chocolate" they think Ghirardelli, and no trip to Fisherman's Wharf is complete without a swing through the Ghirardelli Soda Fountain and Chocolate Shop. Ghirardelli Square is also home to exquisite seafood restaurants and a plethora of shops.

Hyde Street Pier

The historic ferry pier at the end of Hyde Street was once the main auto ferry terminal connecting San Francisco to Marin County, but the opening of the Golden Gate Bridge made car ferrying obsolete. Now, the pier is part of the San Francisco Maritime National Historical Park.

Hyde Street Pier Ships

Notable historic ships like *Balclutha*, *Alma*, and *Eureka* line Hyde Street Pier. Not just for street-side sightseeing, visitors can actually climb aboard several of the ships for guided tours that offer a glimpse into San Francisco's rich maritime history as a major port along the Pacific Coast.

Aquatic Park

Within the San Francisco Maritime National Historic Park, Aquatic Park Cove is often crowded with visitors strolling Hyde Street Pier and locals using the convenient bike paths to commute and recreate along the sunny shore of the Bay.

Balclutha *(top and bottom)*

From Hyde Street Pier, take a tour of the permanently-moored 1886 sailing ship *Balclutha* (formerly the *Pacific Queen*), the only square rigged ship that remains in San Francisco Bay. A National Historic Landmark, this three-masted, steel-hulled ship once lugged cargo around the world.

Marina District

San Francisco's northernmost neighborhood boasts prime waterfront real estate right on the Bay, in full view of the Golden Gate Bridge and the Marin Headlands to the north. Just beyond this serene scene lies a bustling business district where locals love to eat, drink, and shop.

San Francisco Marina

The oldest recreational marina still operating in San Francisco is crowded with small craft occupying 725 berths, providing the perfect launching point for a sail across the Bay and under the Golden Gate Bridge. But beware of the fog; it tends to creep in, particularly on a summer day.

S.S. Jeremiah O'Brien *(opposite, top)*

Eager for a glimpse of the early 20th-century sailor's life? The S.S. *Jeremiah O'Brien* is the last unaltered and historically preserved Liberty ship of the 2,700 built during World War II. Still fully seaworthy, the ship took a commemorative tour to England and France in 1994.

U.S.S. Pampanito *(opposite, bottom)*

This U.S. Navy ship, a Balao-class submarine, saw plenty of service during World War II and sunk six Imperial Japanese ships. Now, the *Pampanito*—named after the pompano fish—is a National Historic Landmark, retired at Fisherman's Wharf, that still sees over 100,000 visitors a year.

Ocean Beach *(above)*

Where the far western edge of San Francisco meets the wild Pacific, Ocean Beach occupies a 3.5-mile stretch of sand and surf. Popular among local surfers and seabirds, the water is generally too cold to swim without a wetsuit, but it's still the perfect spot to take a stroll.

Immigration Station

Between 1910 and 1940, about 175,000 Chinese immigrants came to San Francisco via Immigration Station on Angel Island. While detained for long periods of time during their interrogations, many carved frustrated poetry into the wooden walls of the barracks.

Immigration Station Fog Bell

Immigration Station's two-ton fog bell recalls Angel Island's history as a port of entry for thousands of Asian immigrants, whose descendants make up a large part of the Bay Area's population and culture. The bell has been restored and still serves as a marker at China Cove.

View from Ocean Beach *(top)*

Ocean Beach is often "socked in" with fog, but on the occasional bright and sunny day, locals take advantage of this charming urban strip of sand. In the distance lie Cliff House and the Marin Headlands.

Cliff House *(bottom and opposite)*

Perched on a cliff above Ocean Beach, Cliff House is the place to catch the sunset over a glass of wine. Built in 1858 and stunningly renovated in 2004, its floor-to-ceiling windows offer breath-taking views of the majestic Pacific while sheltering diners from wind and fog.

GIANT CAMERA

Hearts in San Francisco *(top and bottom)*

Since 2004, San Francisco General Heart Foundation has sponsored the creative fundraising project Heroes & Hearts. Artists are invited to submit designs, and the 26 winners see their heart sculptures—or "heartworks"—installed around the city after an official unveiling.

Seven Sisters

A symbol of the city's creative spirit, the spectacular "Painted Ladies" reflect the golden light along one of the city's famous hills. Beyond the vibrantly hued Victorians lies a panoramic view of the skyline, including the Transamerica Pyramid and the Bank of America Center.

Haight Ashbury

The epicenter of the 1960s counterculture, Haight Ashbury is still a magnet for young rebels, with its bohemian shops and cafés harkening back to the Summer of Love. Today, "the Haight," also includes a lovely, gentrified residential neighborhood with soft-hued Victorians lining quiet streets.

Intersection of Haight and Ashbury

Haight and Ashbury streets collide in the heart of the Haight Ashbury District, where one can lazily stroll along perhaps the most famous streets of the 1960s. Long a magnet for the wild and carefree, this is a neighborhood that refuses to grow up.

Shopping in Haight Ashbury *(above)*

For the most far-out shopping experience in San Francisco, visit Haight Ashbury's headshops, costume stores, and quirky boutiques. Piedmont Boutique, with its imaginative second story display, sells fetish wear, feather boas, rhinestones, and wigs for any occasion.

Dining in Haight Ashbury *(opposite)*

Dining in Haight Ashbury tends toward the healthy, but the more adventurous can enjoy a smorgasbord of Mediterranean, Mexican, Thai, Italian, Indian, and French cuisine. In most markets and cafés, like this one, the bohemian influence is clear and the dress code quite laidback.

HAIGHT STREET
MARKET
HAIGHT STREET MARKET

Haas Lilienthal House

San Francisco is known for lovely homes, but only this historic Victorian is open to the public. In 1886, the Haas Lilienthal House on Franklin Street was built of redwood and fir in the Queen Anne style, including a "witches cap" roof which survived the earthquakes of 1906 and 1989.

McElroy Octagon House

A whimsical relic from the briefly popular octagonal architectural style of the mid-1800s, the McElroy House in Cow Hollow once lay on the other side of Gough Street. It was relocated and restored by the Colonial Dames of America in 1951, and is now an official San Francisco landmark.

Beach Chalet *(above)*

The Beach Chalet Brewery & Restaurant is a great spot for a seaside sunset at happy hour. But the real attraction is the downstairs entry hall and its well-preserved frescoes by Lucien Labaudt, a recipient of a 1930s government stimulus program to fund local artists.

Barbary Coast Trail *(left)*

A walking tour connects 20 historic sites and museums from San Francisco's background of gold seekers, railroad barons, beat poets, shanghai kidnappers, and silver kings. Along an almost four-mile route that winds through the city, 180 bronze medallions and arrows mark the way.

16th Avenue Tiled Steps *(opposite)*

A hidden gem in the Sunset District, a vibrant mosaic of tiles embedded in 163 steps paints a vivid sea-to-sky landscape, created by artists Aileen Barr and Colette Crutcher along with community volunteers. Climbing these steps is an aesthetic experience as well as a brisk bout of exercise.

Lombard Street

Lauded as "the crookedest street in the world," this single block of Lombard Street runs one way through Russian Hill at a steep pitch. Along with being a relative thrill to navigate by car or on foot, this block contains some of the city's most gorgeous landscaping and spectacular views.

Filbert Steps

Rampant hills make San Francisco a prime city for pedestrian staircases. Climbing from the Financial District all the way to Telegraph Hill, the wooden Filbert Steps pass through a series of beautiful gardens and spectacular art-deco-style buildings before culminating at Coit Tower.

Embarcadero Center *(opposite)*

This cluster of six interconnected towers in the financial district is a one-stop-shop for retail, restaurants, and events. With two hotels, a movie theater, and offices for 14,000 people, you can find virtually anything you need at the Embarcadero Center—even ice skating, in season.

Outdoor Dining and Shopping at Embarcadero Center *(top and bottom)*

The arches, stairways, and walkways that connect the Embarcadero Center towers provide a lovely al fresco dining and shopping experience—and the occasional glimpse at the Ferry Building Clock Tower just beyond Embarcadero Four.

Dewey Monument

Commemorating Admiral George Dewey's naval victory at the Battle of Manila Bay during the Spanish-American War, Dewey Monument, erected in 1903, features a woman holding a victorious trident and a wreath to honor the memory of U.S. President William McKinley.

Union Square

When San Franciscans say "Union Square," they might mean downtown's high-end shopping district, but technically the name refers to the 2.6-acre public plaza ringed by high-end department stores and boutiques. The plaza is a gathering place where artists often sell their work.

Pacific-Union Club *(above)*

On California Street, at the top of Nob Hill, the Pacific-Union clubhouse was originally home to silver magnate James Clair Flood. The highly secretive, men-only Pacific-Union Club is closed to the public and rumored to follow the dictate "No women, no Democrats, no reporters."

Pioneer Monument *(opposite)*

Created by Frank Happersberger and located in the Civic Center area, controversy has long surrounded this Victorian monument to California's early settlers, whose missionary efforts ultimately resulted in the demise of about half of the Native American population.

SUTTER
FREMONT
IN "49"

Palace of Fine Arts *(top and bottom)*

Constructed for the 1915 Panama-Pacific Exposition as an art gallery, this Roman and Greek–inspired building near the Marina Green is a photogenic spot for picnics, proposals, and weddings. It's also home to the Palace of Fine Arts Theatre, which hosts year-round cultural events.

Palace of Fine Arts Lagoon

Designed to mirror the palace, the lagoon is surrounded by Japanese and Douglas iris, willow trees, sword ferns, and fragrant eucalyptus. This peaceful body of water is inhabited by many forms of wildlife including geese, turtles, and frogs.

Mission Dolores Interior *(top and bottom)*

Known for its beautiful artwork, Mission Dolores was sturdily built with adobe walls, timber, and rawhide. Many of the original roof tiles and hand-carved altars are still in place in the Basilica and Old Mission, along with paintings imported from Mexico over 200 years ago.

Mission Dolores *(opposite)*

Still an active church, Mission San Francisco de Asís is the oldest standing structure in the city and a poignant monument to the city's Spanish heritage. First founded in 1776, it was named for St. Francis but colloquially referred to as Mission Dolores, a geographical reference to a nearby creek.

Asian Art Museum *(above)*

A handsome feat of architecture in the Beaux-Arts style, the Asian Art Museum's real beauty lies within, where one of the most vast collections of Asian art is housed. Visitors immerse themselves in a rich gamut of culture and history, including the oldest known dated Chinese Buddha in the world.

Painted Heart Sculpture *(left)*

San Francisco General Hospital's Heroes & Hearts annual fundraising project adds to the city's tradition of eclectic and colorful outdoor art. Lush, hand-painted hearts like this one, designed by local artists, pop up around the town in the least likely of spots, and no two are alike.

Maritime Museum

Built in 1939 to resemble an ocean liner, the old public bathhouse in Aquatic Park now hosts the San Francisco Maritime Museum, a National Park that displays WPA-era murals of the 1930s, depicting a fantasy underwater world full of sea creatures in dreamy pastels.

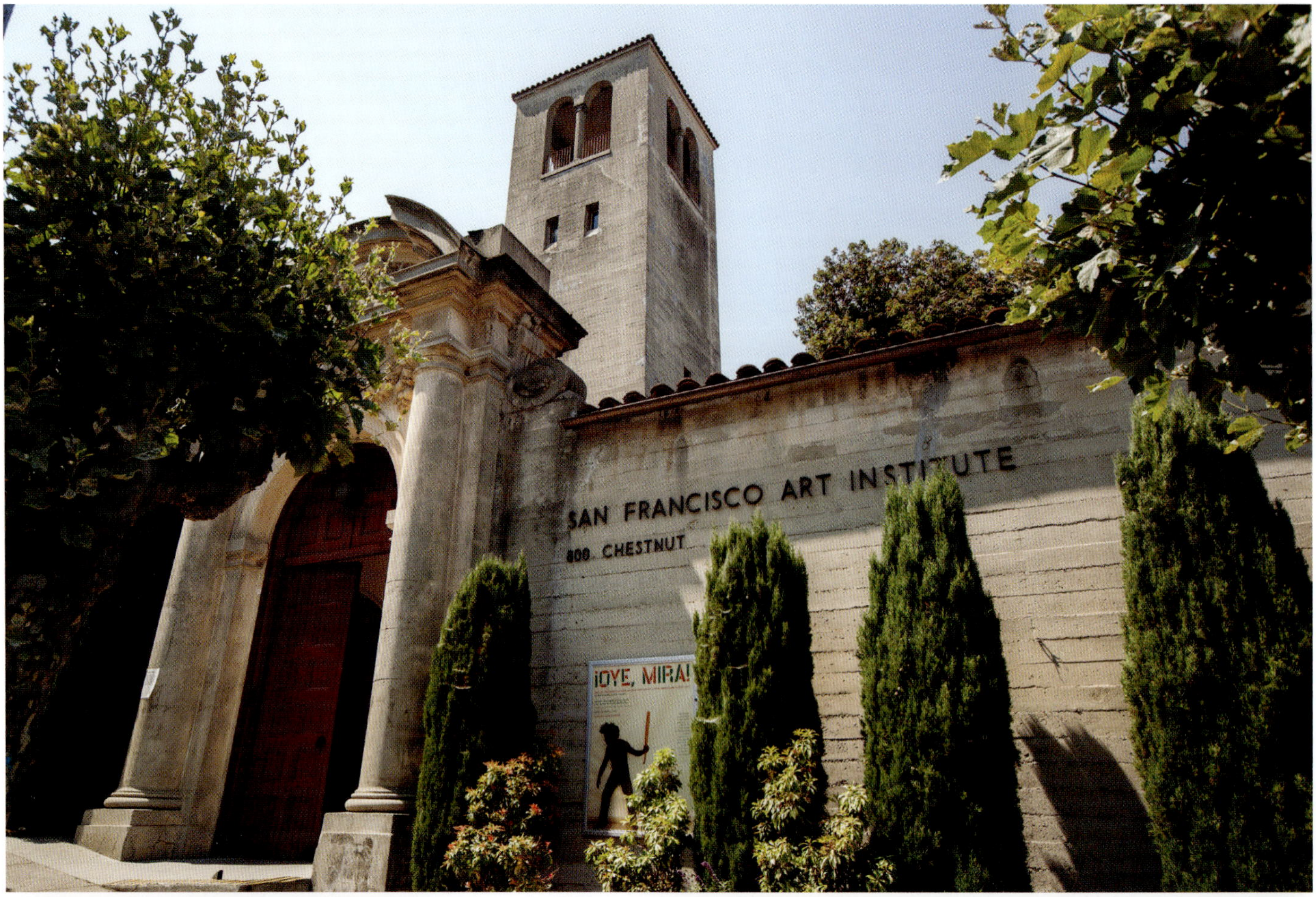
SAN FRANCISCO ART INSTITUTE
800 CHESTNUT
¡OYE, MIRA!

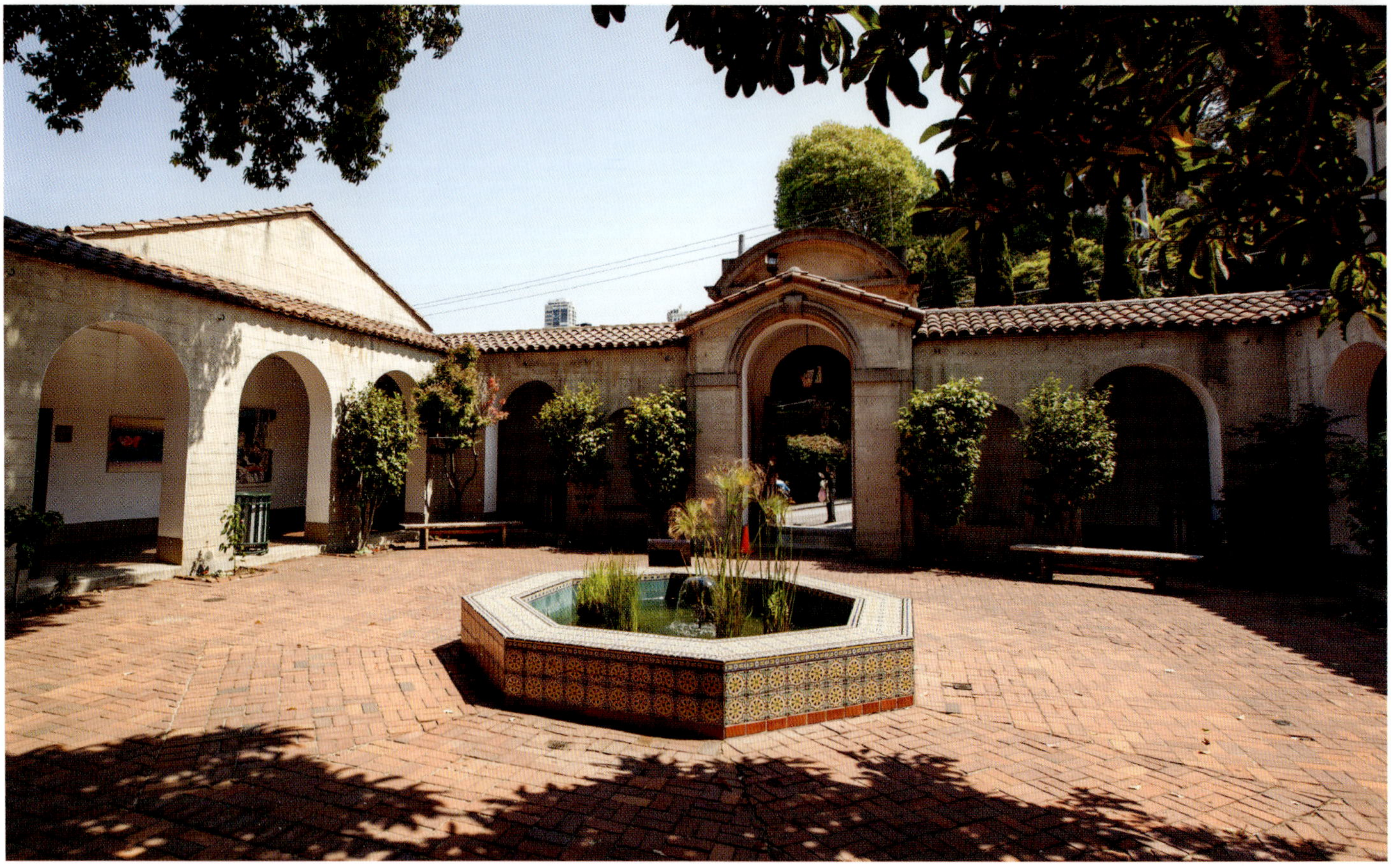

San Francisco Art Institute *(opposite)*

San Francisco Art Institute is a premier school of higher education in contemporary art. The main campus in Russian Hill includes Spanish Colonial Revival buildings that have hosted artists Mark Rothko, Eadweard Muybridge, Annie Leibovitz, Diego Rivera, and Richard Diebenkorn.

Walt Disney Family Museum *(above)*

The former Presidio military base has allowed a few choice institutions to move into the Main Post's historic brick buildings, including the Walt Disney Family Museum, with its ten galleries, a state-of-the-art digital theater, countless artifacts, and Walt Disney's 248 career awards.

Children's Creativity Museum *(top)*

One of the many interactive attractions of Yerba Buena Gardens is the Children's Creativity Museum, a multimedia arts and technology center for kids. "Museum" is a bit of a misnomer, as this inventive educational center is more of a creative, hands-on hangout for children of all ages.

Cable Car Museum *(opposite, top)*

San Francisco's Cable Car Museum is grand central for the antique trolleys that once served as the main form of public transportation in this city. The rich heritage of the cable cars began back in 1873. The museum showcases historic relics and lots of take-home tchotchkes.

Cable Car Turnaround *(opposite, bottom)*

The quaint Powell Street Cable Car Turnaround at Market Street draws plenty of gawkers as well as tourists eager to hitch a ride up steep Powell Street to Nob Hill and all the way down the other side to Fisherman's Wharf.

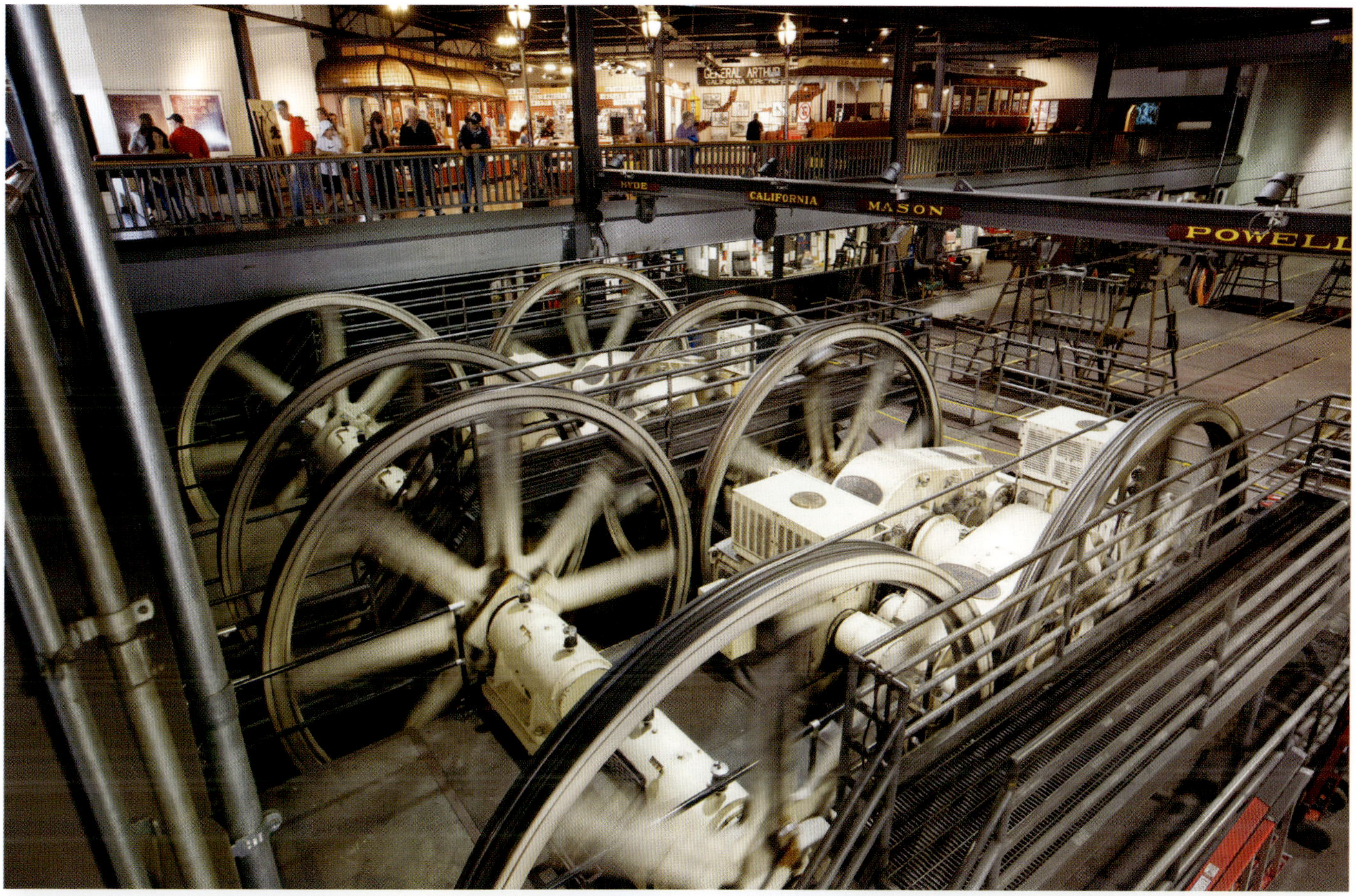
HYDE
CALIFORNIA
MASON

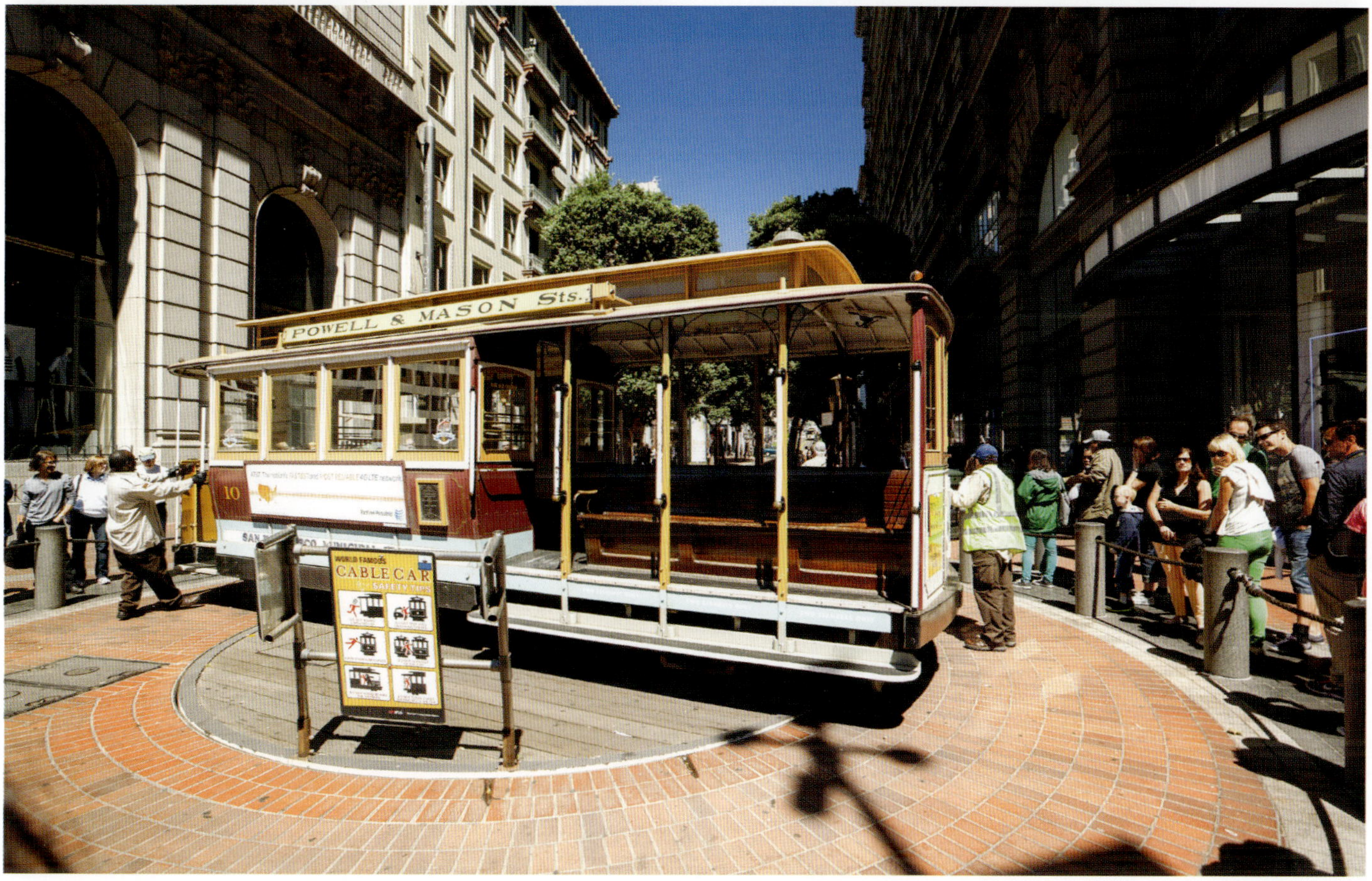
POWELL & MASON Sts.
10
CABLE CAR

Louise M. Davies Symphony Hall

Acoustically superior home of the San Francisco Symphony, Louise M. Davies Hall's modern but cozy circular space comfortably seats 2,743 for performances by the city's beloved symphony. Henry Moore's *Large Four Piece Reclining Figure* is on display outside the hall.

California Academy of Sciences

Golden Gate Park's Academy of Sciences isn't just a state-of-the-art natural history museum with impressive exhibits that range from a living four-story rainforest to an otherworldly planetarium; it's also the cosmopolitan setting for the museum's weekly Nightlife social events for adults.

Wells Fargo Museum *(top)*

On the very site where Wells Fargo & Company opened their first bank in 1852, the Wells Fargo Museum tells tales of the prospectors who settled San Francisco, a city founded on adventurous principles, a willingness to take risks, and a lust for gold.

Wells Fargo Stagecoach *(bottom and opposite)*

The Wells Fargo Museum proudly displays an original Wells Fargo stagecoach, once used to ferry passengers and gold across the West…slowly. Stagecoaches travelled about five miles an hour, with up to nine people crowded inside for an often dusty, bumpy ride across the new frontier.

WELLS FARGO & COMPANY.

4th of July *(top)*

July fourth is a raucous holiday in San Francisco, where locals gather on rooftops and the hills to watch the electrifying fireworks, launched from barges near Fisherman's Wharf and from the foot of Municipal Pier. Other events include live music and entertainment at Pier 39.

Levi Strauss & Co. *(bottom and opposite)*

The iconic San Francisco brand originally sold dry goods that ranged from buttons to bedding, but jeans made the company its name. With an 1873 U.S. patent on riveted denim pants for men, Levi's became an early American trendsetter. This museum commemorates its coolness.

1937
1944
1947
1954
1955
1966

Fire Department Museum *(above and left)*

In a city that was nearly destroyed in the major earthquake and fire of 1906, it's no wonder the fire department is a revered institution. Touring visitors see antique engines and firefighting artifacts with free admission, and the enthusiastic volunteer staff is happy to recount San Francisco's fire department heroics.

Volunteer Firemen Memorial *(opposite)*

This 1933 bronze tribute to the early volunteer firefighters of San Francisco stands proudly in busy Washington Square at the edge of North Beach. It was built with money bequeathed to the city by Lillie Hitchcock Coit, whose legacy also includes the funding of nearby Coit Tower.

FIRE DEPARTMENT
1866
ERECTED 1933
BEQUEST OF
HITCHCOCK COIT

NORTH BEACH
CUCINA TOSCANA
SAN FRANCISCO
RESTAURANT
NORTH BEACH RESTAURANT
CUCINA 1512 TOSCANA
NORTH BEACH RESTAURANT
Dinner
ZAGAT
2013

North Beach *(opposite)*

In San Francisco's version of Little Italy, the city's best lasagna and cannoli can be found in countless comfy, family-style restaurants and cafés. But it's not all about the food; North Beach's heritage is also steeped in Barbary Coast lore and the foundations of the beatnik movement.

Yoda Fountain *(above)*

Captivating visitors at Lucasfilm headquarters in Letterman Digital Arts Center in the restored Presidio is the whimsical *Yoda Fountain*, an ode to a cinematic favorite. This "life-size" statue guards over the front entrances of Lucasfilm, dispensing imaginary wisdom atop a fountain.

San Francisco Botanical Garden

(opposite, top and bottom)

With the city's mild Mediterranean climate and lack of punctuated seasons, the Botanical Garden provides a versatile panoply of year-round flora. Over 8,000 different types of plants from around the world populate the serene landscape.

Conservatory of Flowers *(above)*

For those with a yen for the extraordinary, this quixotic domed structure in Golden Gate Park is a historic wooden greenhouse that holds a collection of rare and exotic plants: orchids, water lilies, philodendron, and even butterflies abound in this hothouse of terrestrial beauty.

Japanese Tea Garden *(above and opposite, top)*

Golden Gate Park's Japanese Tea Garden is the oldest public Japanese tea garden in the country. Built in 1894 as part of the California Midwinter International Exposition of the World's Fair, it is a favorite place for those seeking a Zen experience among the pagodas and koi ponds.

Japanese Tea Garden Buddha *(right)*

The Japanese Tea Garden's resident Buddha, over 200 years old and imported from Japan, presides over a small enclosed park of immaculately designed walkways and wooden bridges. Here, architecture meets landscape in an aesthetic Eastern display of harmony and tranquility. Don't miss the tea house for the complete experience.

Muir Woods *(above and opposite)*

North of the city, Muir Woods National Monument is the perfect place to mingle among California's legendary redwoods. From the visitor center, a series of walkways and interpretive signs aid in the natural experience while preserving the sanctity of the wilderness.

Great Redwoods *(pages 98 –99)*

The namesake of Muir Woods, John Muir, was dedicated to the preservation of California's wilderness. His mission has been carried on by the National Park Service, who host a million visitors a year under a canopy of redwoods that can reach 250 feet and 1,200 years old.

Bridge

Golden Gate National Recreation Area

Golden Gate National Recreation Area encompasses over 80,000 acres, including the Marin Headlands, which slope majestically from the Golden Gate Bridge to Pt. Reyes in a series of trails, beaches, and coves once frequented by Coast Miwok and now by hikers, bikers, and surfers.

Don Quixote

This imaginative bronze and stone statue of chivalrous fictional character Don Quixote and his sidekick Sancho Panza kneeling at the feet of their creator, Miguel de Cervantes Saavedra, is a cheeky tribute to a famed story. It is located just off JFK Drive in Golden Gate Park.

Herschell-Spillman Carousel *(above)*

Golden Gate Park's colorful 1914 carousel was once steam powered but was eventually converted to electric, thanks to the generosity of PG&E. Sixty-two animal figures have received various touch-ups over the years, so the carousel is still a colorful place to take a whirl.

Dutch Windmill *(opposite)*

Ocean Beach-goers might notice a whimsical windmill perched nearby. Once a functional energy generator for the city, capturing the westerly winds to pump hundreds of gallons of water a day, the 75-foot-tall windmill is now a historic gem enhanced by a rotating floral display.

Francis Scott Key *(above)*

The American poet who penned the lyrics to *The Star-Spangled Banner* is memorialized in Golden Gate Park's Music Concourse. Interestingly, the monument was unveiled in 1888, forty-three years before *The Star-Spangled Banner* reached anthem status.

Beethoven *(opposite)*

Famed German composer Ludwig van Beethoven is memorialized in this bronze statue in the Music Concourse in Golden Gate Park. The head of the celebrated composer dominates over a female figure holding a lyre, a classical stringed instrument popular in ancient Greece.

BEETHOVEN

Fleet Week Blue Angels

A highlight of the Bay Area fall is the annual Fleet Week air show, when the Blue Angels perform their daredevil stunts for a captivated audience on the ground. As the planes roar overhead, many also take to the Bay in sailboats and small craft ideal for open sky viewing.

Fog

Locals call it being "socked in" by the "Marine layer," a weather phenomenon that often ensconces the Golden Gate Bridge and pockets of the city in a thick, moody nest of fog, especially in the summer, sometimes the coolest part of the year in the Bay Area.

Sailing *(above and opposite, top)*

San Francisco is a sailors' town. On days blustery to serene, private and chartered boats crowd the Bay for tours around Alcatraz Island, Angel Island, and Treasure Island, and all the way under the Golden Gate Bridge to the open ocean just beyond.

Sightseeing Boats *(bottom)*

Anchored at Pier 43 ½, the Red and White Fleet has two sightseeing boats that take up to 300 passengers at a time for a cruise on the Bay, a great way to catch the sun setting over the Pacific and a twilight view of the sparkling San Francisco skyline.

Point Bonita Lighthouse
(opposite, top and bottom)

A lookout point at the entrance to the San Francisco Bay, Point Bonita is still actively maintained by the U.S. Coast Guard and open to visitors. It's a somewhat steep but picturesque trek for those parked in the lot about a half mile away.

Sailing the Golden Gate *(above)*

The strait that links the Pacific to San Francisco Bay is called Golden Gate, thus the bridge's moniker. A sail under the Golden Gate Bridge is a highlight of any seaworthy outdoorsman's trip to the Bay Area, as well as of the many cruise ships that sail into the Bay.

Chinatown *(above and left)*

Brightly colored buildings with baroque flourishes are typical in San Francisco's bustling Chinese district, the oldest and largest Chinatown in North America. The city's population is more than 20 percent Chinese-American, providing for a great place to spend an afternoon exploring eclectic markets, tea houses, and temples.

Shopping in Chinatown

Chinatown's many emporiums stock fare that runs the gamut from Chinese-themed plastic kitsch to authentic mementos found nowhere else. Cloth lanterns, woks, Buddha statues, rice bowls, imported tea leaves, and Kung-Fu shoes are just some of the available retail delights.

Three Monkeys *(above)*

The statue of the *Three Wise Monkeys* at 433 Grant Avenue illustrates the proverb "See no evil, hear no evil, speak no evil," and the accompanying bench leaves room for pedestrians to be part of the art. This pictorial maxim dates back to a 17th-century Japanese carving.

Japantown *(left)*

While significantly smaller than Chinatown, San Francisco's Japantown is still the biggest and oldest Japantown in the U.S., spanning six square blocks, at the periphery of which is perched the Japan Center Pagoda. Visit the Japan Center for a bite of sushi or to cruise the many boutiques.

Goddess of Democracy *(opposite)*

A replica of the original *Goddess of Democracy* statue, which was built by Tiananmen Square protestors in Beijing in 1989 and soon after destroyed by soldiers, is dedicated to those who strive for human rights and democracy. The 600-pound bronze monument stands in Chinatown's Portsmouth Square.

Farmers Market *(opposite, top)*

Three times a week, throngs of local farmers and food purveyors fill the Ferry Building plaza for the best, biggest, and most lively farmers market in the city. About 25,000 people visit the market weekly to shop, eat, and learn about food from local chefs and culinary luminaries.

Vaillancourt Fountain *(opposite, bottom)*

Installed in a prominent spot on the downtown waterfront just across from the Ferry Building, this bold sculpture features a second story catwalk and large stepping stones that allow visitors to walk through the roaring water.

Ferry Building *(above)*

The historic San Francisco Ferry Building is far more than just the terminal for commuter ferries. Originally opened in 1898, it was ambitiously renovated in the 2000s and is now a bustling hub of tourist activity, artisan food, fine dining, and wine tasting along its central nave.

Oakland Bay Bridge *(pages 116 – 117)*

The San Francisco-Oakland Bay Bridge connects Oakland to San Francisco in two spans. The brand new easterly span connects Oakland to Treasure Island. The older, western span (pictured) gracefully lights up the night over the Bay.

AT&T Park *(top and bottom)*

Home of the Giants, AT&T Park is San Francisco's monument to Major League Baseball. Opened in 2000 to replace the aging Candlestick Park, AT&T Park also hosts occasional sporting and music events in the off season. Fans arrive by car, Muni, ferry, kayak, or on foot.

AT&T Park's Giants *(opposite)*

Baseball is more than the national pastime in San Francisco; it's practically an obsession. Get any local talking about their beloved Giants and you'll find they have a lot to say. AT&T Park can accommodate 41,503 such enthusiastic fans per game.

AT&T PARK
AT&T PARK
HOME OF THE SAN FRANCISCO GIANTS
WILLIE MAYS GATE

Juan Marichal *(above)*

Outside AT&T Park is a statue of Juan Antonio Marichal Sánchez, a legendary Giants pitcher known for his high leg-kick and his intimidation tactics with batters. Born in the Dominican Republic, Marichal played for the Giants from 1960–1973 before moving on to the Red Sox and then the Dodgers.

Willie Mays *(left)*

Originally named Pacific Bell Park and then renamed AT&T Park, many fans casually refer to the stadium as "Mays Field" in honor of legend Willie Mays, a one-time center fielder for the Giants who shares the record of most All-Star Games played with Hank Aaron and Stan Musial.

Canoes in McCovey Cove *(above)*

Aquatically daring fans can arrive at AT&T Park on rental kayaks from nearby South Beach Harbor. It's only a quick ten-minute paddle into McCovey Cove, and the rare fan that catches a home-run ball from the water—a "splash hit"—seals his bragging rights for good.

Willie McCovey Statue *(right)*

Famous Giants first baseman and left-handed batter is the namesake for McCovey Cove and the inspiration for this statue. Plaques around the statue list winners of the Willie Mac Award, given annually to the player who displays the spirit and leadership qualities Willie McCovey was known for in his time.

Cherry Blossom Festival *(top)*

Japanese-American culture and community is celebrated joyfully during the annual Northern California Cherry Blossom Festival in Japantown. Sample udon and teriyaki, take part in a chanoyu (tea ceremony), and admire the vibrant, spirited floats in the Grand Parade.

Bay to Breakers *(bottom)*

San Francisco is eternally free spirited, so it's no surprise that this annual footrace, from San Francisco Bay to Ocean Beach, is half legitimate race, half saucy parade of costumed participants in various states of undress and inebriation.

Queen and Her Court

The Grand Parade of the Northern California Cherry Blossom Festival begins at the Civic Center and winds its way to Japantown, where the Queen and her Court bask in the adoration of thousands of visitors, making this Cherry Blossom Festival second in size only to Washington D.C.'s.

Dentzel Carousel *(above)*

San Francisco Zoo's Dentzel Carousel is a functioning historic artifact, one of the last existing machines hand-crafted by William H. Dentzel in the 1920s. Its menagerie of hand-carved wooden characters includes horses, giraffes, tigers, lions, and ostriches.

San Francisco Zoo *(opposite, top and bottom)*

Tucked away into a serene southwest corner of the city, San Francisco Zoo is an exotic educational getaway where one can catch a glimpse of a grizzly bear or a California sea lion, take an Australian walkabout, or catch a ride on the historic "Little Puffer" miniature steam train.

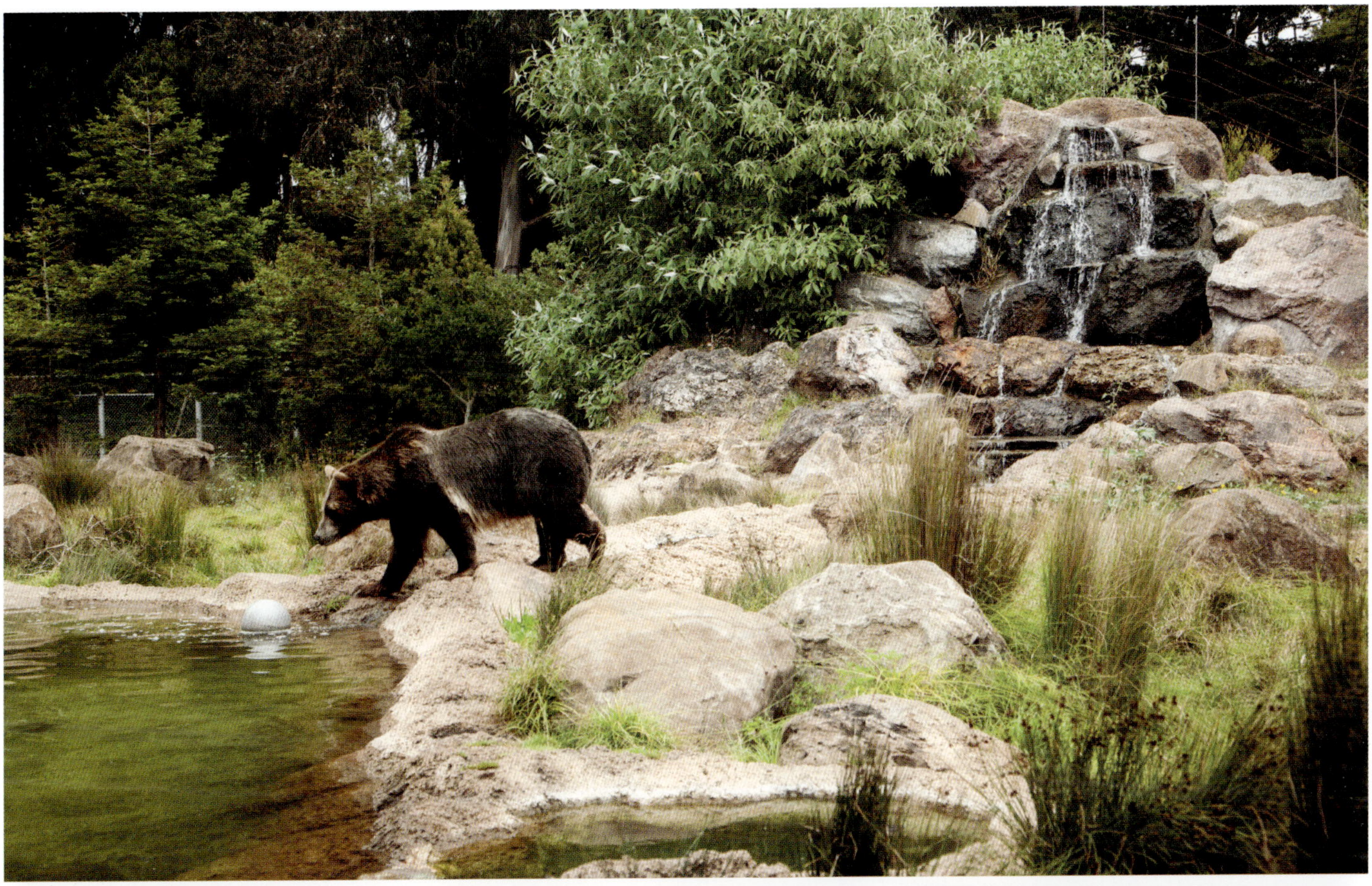

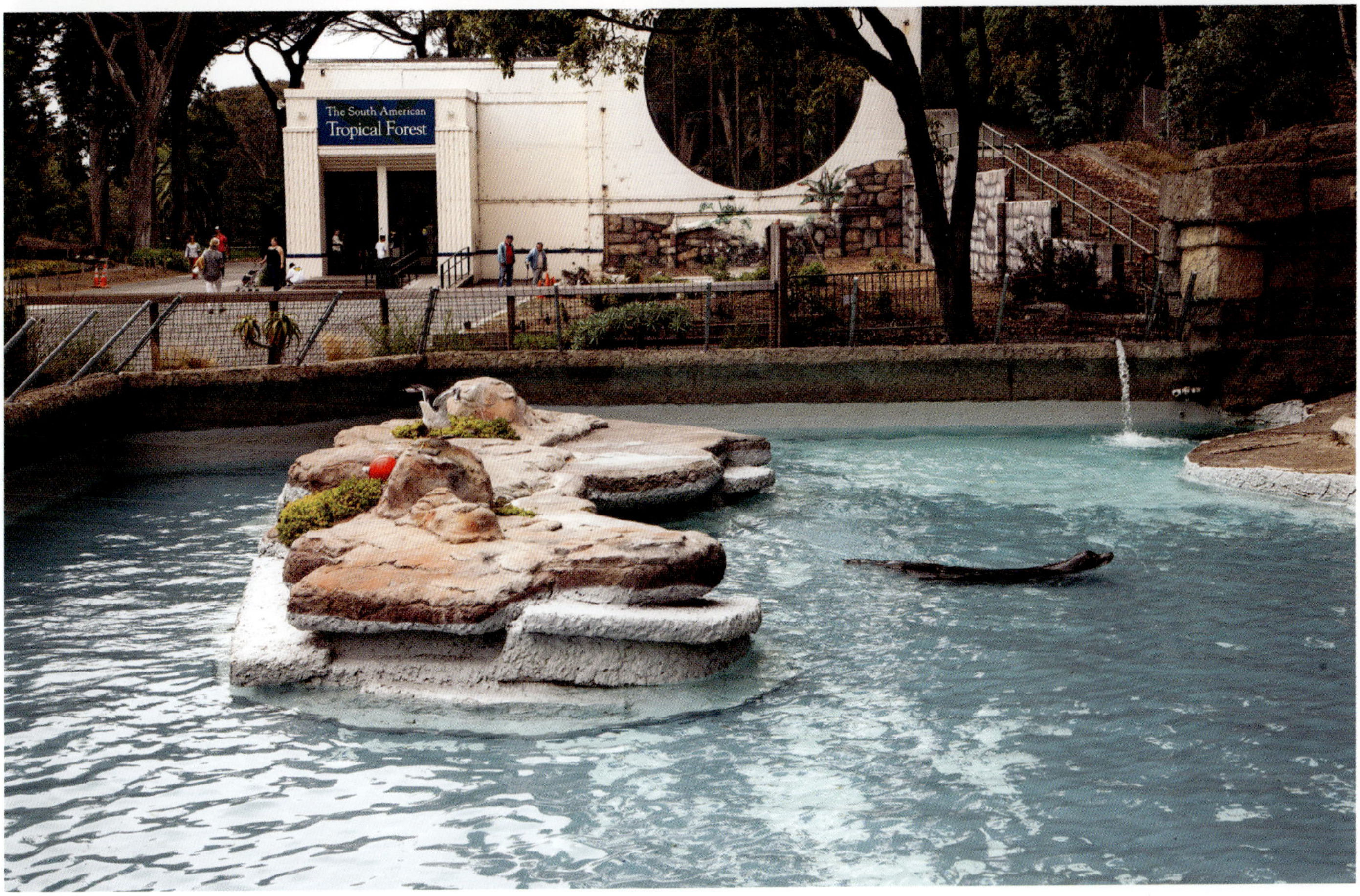
The South American
Tropical Forest

Bob Morris

Bob Morris is a San Francisco Bay Area based photographer specializing in people, architecture, interiors, and stock. With over 25 years' experience, he began his career as a staff photographer for the Southern Pacific Railroad based in San Francisco. With that company's vast land holdings in the western states, assignments were varied and challenging. Included were aerials, logging operations, coal mines, executive portraits, industrial parks, and, of course, trains for the company's public relations, annual reports, advertising, and brochures. Bob now shoots assignments for various clients around the U.S. and adds to his stock library as time allows. To learn more about Bob, please visit www.bobmorrisphoto.com and www.sfstockphoto.com.

Joslyn Hamilton

A lifelong writer by nature, Joslyn Hamilton parlayed her passion for words into a freelance copywriting business, Outside Eye Consulting, and has also written for various publications including *NYTimes.com, McSweeney's Internet Tendency, Common Ground,* and *Elephant Journal.* She has edited and ghostwritten books on a variety of themes such as cooking, poetry, personal finance, and yoga. She is the co-founder and co-managing editor of the irreverent website RecoveringYogi.com as well as a frequent contributor to the site.

Joslyn lives, writes, and hikes through the merciless Bay Area fog from her home in Marin County, just north of the always breathtaking Golden Gate Bridge. Her unflagging reverence for the many sights and landscapes of San Francisco and the surrounding countryside stem from her chilly upbringing in cold, blustery New England. To read more of Joslyn's writing, visit www.outsideeyeconsulting.com.